Richard Martin

The Four Seasons

The Costume Institute / The Metropolitan Museum of Art

This volume has been published in conjunction with the exhibition "The Four Seasons," held at The Metropolitan Museum of Art, New York, from April 8, 1997, to August 17, 1997.

The exhibition is made possible by **DuPont Tactel nylon.**

Published by The Metropolitan Museum of Art, New York
Copyright © 1997 The Metropolitan Museum of Art

John P. O'Neill, Editor in Chief
Barbara Cavaliere, Editor
Russ Kane, Design
Richard Bonk, Production

Costume photography by Karin L. Willis, The Photograph Studio, The Metropolitan Museum of Art

ISBN 0-87099-792-0
Printed by Meridian Printing Company, East Greenwich, Rhode Island

Sponsor's Statement

It is a great honor for DuPont Tactel to sponsor "The Four Seasons" exhibition at The Costume Institute of The Metropolitan Museum of Art. With the emergence of year-round dressing, a phenomenon made possible by the development of modern fibers such as Tactel nylon, it is fitting that DuPont joins The Metropolitan Museum of Art to celebrate fashions designed for spring, summer, fall, and winter, as well as for that "fifth" season, of seasonless dressing. We are pleased to be associated with The Costume Institute's unique, historical reflection on fashion's approach to all seasons.

Robert W. Pruyn
Business Director—Apparel
DuPont Nylon North America

Introduction

> To every thing there is a season, and a time to every purpose under the heavens.
>
> Ecclesiastes, 3:1

Throughout The Metropolitan Museum of Art, works of art assure our perception of the time of year. Universal are such calibrations as we witness spring flowers on a Momoyama sake vessel or the walkers through spring showers in Ukioye prints. We can see *Spring* emulate the early life of a human being in a sixteenth-century Belgian tapestry, and the season is epitomized by the delicate *Pear Blossoms* in a handscroll by Ch'ien Hsüän (ca. 1280). Similarly, summer landscape gently unifies the scroll *Summer Mountains* attributed to Ch'u Ting (ca. 1023-56), and summer sun radiates from Joseph Mallord William Turner's *The Grand Canal, Venice* (1835) and from the brilliant seaside in Claude Monet's *Garden at Sainte-Adresse* (1867). June-intense sun inflames Vincent van Gogh's *Sunflowers* (1887) and *Cypresses* (1889). Late summer gilds the countryside and activity in Pieter Bruegel's *The Harvesters* (1565).

Autumn dark and storm dim the scene in Jean François Millet's *Haystacks: Autumn* (1873-74). Fall's vivacious paintbox tinges the multicolored landscape in the Louis Comfort Tiffany window *Autumn Landscape* (1923) and explodes metaphorically in Jackson Pollock's *Autumn Rhythm* (1950). Winter's blasts chill Emanuel Leutze's *Washington Crossing the Delaware* (1851) and Currier & Ives's *Winter in the Country* (1873), which appeared in American almanacs, even as they do Camille Pissarro's dampness-saturated *The Boulevard Montmartre on a Winter Morning* (1897). At first it is perhaps ironic to realize that the Impressionists who are probably best remembered for their burning canvases of summer heat were also devoted to the environmental, light-changing effects of winter shadows and lustrous snow.

Are these works of art, along with so many other examples, merely the descriptive accounts of a particular time, or are they touchstones to our sensibility, reckonings with the variable light, landscape, and emotions of the seasons, and records of the deep place the seasons occupy in our psyches? In Asia, Europe, and America, there have been traditions of painters representing the seasons and/or the months as part of the disciplined practice of being able to render what is seen but also being able to extrapolate contemplation from observation.

The seasons are our measure of the year, itself a larger unit of transitory and eternal time. The seasons resemble nature's progress through the round of the year, but they in no way, at any point on the meridian, completely encompass the quarter or the whole. "The Four Seasons" examines fashion's intimate relation to the calendar not as an exact record but as an intellectual construct, even a set of hopes that governs time's remorseless progression.

White sales, Easter bonnets, and back-to-school clothes may encourage us to associate fashion's seasonal evolution with commerce, but fashion's parallels to the year's quarterly units are not merely a matter of business incentives. Rather, we appraise our passage through living via the sweet memories, occasions, and apparel peculiar to a season. Like the other artists whose works reside in this Museum, those who have made fashion have not practiced a banal or purely temporal art. Rather, they bring us into accord with the seasons as monitors of our behavior.

In fact, fashion is ill-served by its misalliance with etiquette. If art's allegiance with and accord to the seasons seem deliberate and judicious, fashion's account of the seasons has sometimes seemed ridiculous. Think, for example, of the advice proffered by Judith Martin in *Miss Manners' Guide for the Turn-of-the-Millennium* (1989):

From Memorial Day to Labor Day, you may wear white shoes. Not before and not after. As a command, the White Shoe Edict should be clear and simple enough. Do not violate it. In a society in which everything else has become relative, a matter of how it makes you feel, a question between you and your conscience, and an opportunity for you to be really you, this is an absolute. Miss Manners not only doesn't want any argument about it, she doesn't even want any discussion.

Such a dress rule, codifying season and specific dress, is as improbable in late-twentieth-century reality as it may have once been enforceable in a society of unequivocal and multiple dress-code signifiers, including class, profession, and occasion. Season continues to define our clothing, even after the upending of most of the other Victorianisms, because it is not a society-based system but a natural order that we observe. Miss Manners goes on to say:

Dividing the calendar year into different seasons, one hot, one cold, one chilly, and one romantic, was one of nature's more charming ideas, but it was a vague one. Many perfectly agreeable places to live don't follow that system at all, and even regions that pretend to, enjoy upsetting people occasionally just for a laugh, and schedule heat waves and cold fronts (whatever they are) when they don't belong. Sensible people therefore adhere to the concept of the seasons, without regard to whatever chaotic conditions may be prevailing outdoors.

Fashion's seasons have reasons. They are needful calibrations in the calendar of time. The seasons provide fashion simultaneously with principles of recurrence and of change. Anyone knows the rewards of this system, though its Mother is probably more about Nurture than Nature. Each season's spring wardrobe emerges fresher than ever with its perennially bright hues, but so too nature always comes through with a painterly springtime. Every winter's wardrobe, as it is taken out of mothballs or the attic, seems snuggley and warm, at least through the first blizzards. We return with an enchanted memory to every season, even as we move ahead in the journey of years and years. Tonne Goodman reported in *Harper's Bazaar* (March 1997): "Here's a radical thought: Spring is dead. Cream off the froth that filled much of the airspace at the spring collections, and what you're really looking at is a roster of clothes you could wear at any time of the year." In our tendency to seasonless dressing, we do not discredit the seasons; we acknowledge that contemporary culture remembers them, even as we surpass some of their conventions and climatic conditions.

Years pass quickly. We cannot thwart time, but we can enjoy it through the pleasures of the seasons, foremost among which is fashion. Clothing—its colors, materials, allusions—distinguishes seasons not ultimately to sell us more clothing but to tell us of life's fascinating cycles. "There is," as poet William Browne averred in the seventeenth century, "no season such delight can bring, /As summer, autumn, winter, and the spring."

Spring

Ch'ien Hsüän, *Pear Blossoms* (detail), handscroll, ink and colors on paper, ca. 1280

Spring showers and spring flowers dominate this season's wardrobe, but the season's festive association with fashion—especially the Easter bonnet—renews the wardrobe in accord with nature's apparent rebirth. From the flower-sprouting mantuas of the eighteenth century to the beguiling spring dresses of the 1920s and 1930s, nature's rejuvenation enters into the spirit of spring dress.

As if reenacting Botticelli's *Primavera*, we take on the raiment of soft texture, light weights, and glee, shifting our focus from the layers, density, and interior lifestyle of winter to a single ply, sheerness, and the outdoor lifestyle. Diaphanous dresses suitable to the Graces become spring mufti. Yet spring does not run riot. It has its shipshape regulations as life moves outdoors. Navy-blue and white, especially in France, are often a sign of the season, representing a jaunty nautical optimism.

As early a writer as Catullus noted: "Now spring brings back balmy warmth." The lush flora of springtime is only the sign of nature's bounty substantiated by love and gladness. Spring's reopening of the human body after winter's dense wrap is as familiar today as it was in the eighteenth century. This poetic awakening is sensual, corresponding to nature's facile procreation, affording the wardrobe some of its most seductive dresses.

As spring's buds of regeneration begin to flower, the apparel of the season moves gradually toward summer, introducing blanched grounds for the multicolored florals of spring; light and a lightness of being are sustained until June's summer solstice.

English, robe à la française, ca. 1765

Summer

Claude Monet,
Garden at Sainte-Adresse,
oil on canvas,
1867

In *The Secrets of Distinctive Dress* (1918), Mary Brooks Picken admitted: "Elderly mothers have come to realize that they look ten years younger and are ten times more comfortable on a warm summer's day in a pretty, soft white dress, and it is pleasing to see a group of such mothers dressed in pretty, light wash dresses as they appear many times as attractive as a group of young women."

Summer is the most joyous and sequestered of all the seasons. With its conventions of straw hats, white shoes, gingham brights, and fields of white cotton articulated by borders, flowers, or cutwork perforations, summer is the season of fashion's relaxation, but also of fashion's distinction. Recreation and long sun-filled days betoken Impressionist outings and radiant canvases. As Picken intuited, summer seems to favor youth. Light seersuckers, airy cutwork and lace, and the ubiquitous white dress accommodate summer's warmth and sun but also personify a spirit of innocence and delight. Childhood and youth are also associated with this season of school holidays and freedom. Even grownups are afforded the license of men's seersucker suits in fresh blue and white, as evident back to the early years of the nineteenth century, and of the playful tartans that transform winter-wool warmth to summer-cotton cool in bright colors and shine.

If summer is the most extreme season of heat and thus allows for a loosening of some dress codes in contemporary culture, one must remember that light-wool flannel remained popular in women's daywear through the 1950s. Summer is not inherently improper with Huckleberry Finn impudence; it is buoyant with estival liberties, freedom of motion, and lighter colors and materials.

Fall

Louis Comfort
Tiffany, *Autumn
Landscape,*
stained glass,
1923

In fall the landscape is painted and the body is cloaked in soft russets, oranges, leaflike *changeant* burnished golds, deep browns, and earth tones. Friction of materials with the skin is a welcome pleasure as days grow cooler and the more substantial wools, cotton corduroys, and velvets increasingly supplant the lighter, less textural fabrics of summer. Our impression of eighteenth-century dress may lead us to expect silk and décolletage, but the Kimberley gown, an English open robe and petticoat (ca. 1695) in gray-brown-blue wool with silver gilt embroidery, refutes those expectations. On the contrary, the Kimberley gown testifies to seasonal differentiation as early as seventeenth-century dress through its fabric, color, and body coverage. Correspondingly, tan and brown corduroy suits for men and women alike similarly suggest the back-to-school autumnal season. Tartan's woolen warmth and the evocation of Scottish Highlands history also substantiate the fall.

The autumnal colors of tweeds and tenebrous velvets are matched in the materials along with the development of cloaking and wrapping to stave off the cool weather and erratic breezes of the season. As poet Stephen Vincent Benet wrote in his American epic: "The fall with his sachem colors, the summer wind by the shore,/The spring like an Indian runner, beautiful, stripped, and swift,/They knew these things in their season—and yet there was something more/And they thought not only of harvest, when they thanked their God for His gift."

Charles James, cocktail suit, 1951

Winter

Currier & Ives, *Winter Morning in the Country*, lithograph with colors, 1873

The winter wardrobe is an arsenal of techniques for fending off the cold and capturing all available warmth. Quilting creates a natural layer of downy protection, and animal pelts and their simulation in plush provide a cuddly defense against cold winds. Both are eternal verities of the winter wardrobe, extending from eighteenth- and nineteenth-century examples to contemporary fashion.

Winter's defensive dressing, however, is not necessarily directed to a visual differentiation from nature. Winter whites may at first resemble the cool whites of summer, but materials such as eiderdown and ermine create chameleon figures in a snowy landscape. Rich textures, fur trim as reinforcement and insulating perimeter, and layers of weighty wools fortify the body against winter's legendary cold, wind, and storm. Even the calmest winter is vilified for its apparent lack of production in nature and its dormancy. Yet it is in this season that light is restored, and the days lengthen after the winter solstice. Long assembled to shield us against the worst adversity that nature can hurl against us, winter's formidable dress is picturesque and a splendid comfort. Down coats and snowsuits suggest physical warmth, but they are often just as successful in providing a feeling of warm self-confidence.

Last to arrive in the cycle of the calender year, winter yet offers the junction to spring to renew the entire cycle. Thus, a Balenciaga ensemble of skirt and blouse combines the sheer anticipation of spring as a blouse with the fuzz of winter's warmth, as double-conceived as January's dual faces. Winter's recreations hinge on the assurances of dryness and warmth while skating, skiing, sledding, or otherwise traversing the winter landscape. If the season seems to test clothing's mettle, as nature does humankind's, winter is the ultimate season of gentle comforts.

French, dress, ca. 1874

All Seasons

Giovanni di Paolo,
active by 1417-
died 1482,
Paradise,
tempera and gold
on canvas

The seasons have established their conventions, and the passages of light and temperature can govern some behaviors, but contemporary fashion has yielded to a new principle of seasonless dressing. Of course, the model is not wholly new. The utility of accompanying an Empire gown of sheer cotton with a wool Kashmir or Paisley shawl was a logical compromise as early as the 1800s. Travel, controlled environments, and ever more versatile fibers and fabrics encourage us to live beyond the seasons and to become men and women for all seasons.

If we are thus capable of subduing and surpassing nature, do we wholly live beyond seasons, or do we remember that they were not only substantial, but also intangible, quadrants to our lives and thinking? Their

principles, sometimes quaint, sometimes inhibiting, were not wholly irrational. The seasons we will never abandon are not the extremes of color and fabric or the etiquettes of dress appropriate to one season or another but the memory and chronicle of a year's passage. We live in time and register days, months, seasons, and years in continuity with our remembrance of what we have known before and our desire to see harmony and predictability in what we learn in evolving time. Philosopher Gilles Lipovetsky sees fashion as inexorable novelty, unrelentingly new and uncertain. But the new is conditional on the known and may be rotation and renewal as much as novelty. Fashion is a comfort, a reminder of times we have enjoyed and a hope for sweet memories in the time that unfolds before us.

Yamamoto and Gaultier,

sweater dresses,

1993-94

Notes to the Illustrations

Note. All the works of art in this publication are in the collection of The Metropolitan Museum of Art, and all the costumes are in The Costume Institute/The Metropolitan Museum of Art.

Cover. Jackson Pollock, *Autumn Rhythm: Number 30, 1950* (detail), 1950. Oil on canvas, 105 x 207 in. (266.7 x 525.8 cm). George A. Hearn Fund, 1957 (57.92)

Spring
Ch'ien Hsüan, *Pear Blossoms* (detail), Yüan Dynasty (1279-1368), ca. 1280. Handscroll, ink and colors on paper, 12¼ x 37½ in. (31.1 x 95.3 cm). Purchase, The Dillon Fund Gift, 1977 (1977.79)

English, open robe and petticoat (robe à la française), ca. 1765. Yellow Spitalfields silk brocaded with polychrome floral garlands and bouquets. Purchase, Irene Lewisohn Bequest, 1975 (1975.206.2 a,b)

> This flaxen eighteenth-century dress with chest-baring décolletage and flourishes of floral bouquets suggests the celebratory and gala aspects of court dress.

Summer
Claude Monet, *Garden at Sainte-Adresse,* 1867. Oil on canvas, 38⅝ x 51⅛ in. (98.1 x 129.9 cm). Purchase, special contributions and funds given or bequeathed by friends of the Museum, 1967 (67.241)

American, promenade dress, 1862-64. White cotton piqué trimmed with black soutash braid. Gift of Chauncey Stillman, 1960 (CI 60.6.11 a,b)

> The wide compass of 1860s dress was lightened year-round by the crinoline infrastructure. Its summer version is in cool white cotton.

Fall
Louis Comfort Tiffany, *Autumn Landscape,* 1923. Stained glass, 11 ft. x 8 ft. 6 in. Gift of Robert W. de Forest, 1925 (25.173)

Charles James, cocktail suit, 1951. Black cashmere and rust silk satin. Gift of Eleanor Searle Whitney McCollum, 1975 (1975.246.5 a-c)

> Capturing fall's colors, James created a suit of pronounced modernist shapes, complementing cashmere with an orange-rust silk satin.

Winter
Currier & Ives, *Winter Morning in the Country,* 1873. Lithograph with color, 8¾ x 12¾ in. (21.5 x 31.5 cm). Bequest of Adele S. Colgate, 1963 (63.550.120)

French, dress, ca. 1874. Blue silk faille and velvet with silver fox-fur trim. Gift of Mrs. J. Chester Chamberlain, 1952 (CI 52.13.3 b-d)

> Staunch materials begin to appear in the fall, but they are reinforced in winter with plush and fur trims.

All Seasons
Giovanni di Paolo, active by 1417-died 1482, *Paradise* (fragment of a Last Judgment). Tempera and gold on canvas, transferred from wood; overall 18½ x 16 in. (47 x 40.6 cm); painted surface 17½ x 15⅛ in. (44.5 x 38.4 cm). Rogers Fund, 1906 (06.1046)

Left: Yohji Yamamoto, distressed sweater dress, spring-summer 1993. Black cotton knit. Gift of Richard Martin, 1993 (1993.96).
Right: Jean Paul Gaultier, deconstructed sweater dress, fall-winter 1993-94. Black and moss-green acrylic knit. Purchase, Gifts from various donors, 1994 (1994.9.3)

> Sweaters are ostensibly about warmth, but these two of the 1990s are as conceptual as they might be cozy, sacrificing a toasty wrap to a more delicate idea of deconstruction.

Inside covers (back cover reversed). American or European, man's coat, 1795-98 (detail). Blue-and-white striped cotton. Gift of J. C. Hawthorne, 1946 (CI 46.82.16)

> Cotton striped in blue and white has become a convention of summer menswear and womenswear, most often in seersucker. The tradition goes back at least to the eighteenth century.